Junior High
Internet Research Projects (Grades 5-8)

Israel

Use a phone, tablet or laptop to answer these questions.

1. What language do they speak? _____
2. How many people live there? _____
3. How big is this country? _____
4. Who is their leader? _____
5. Where is the capitol? _____
6. What kind of money do they _____
7. How long have they been a na _____
8. What religions are most com _____
9. What sport is most popular? _____

10. What are three interesting th _____
_____
_____
_____
_____

SOURCE: _____
SOURCE: _____
SOURCE: _____

Becoming a scientist

What does it take to _____
Use a computer, tablet or phone to se _____

1 _____
2 _____
3 _____
5 _____

ONLINE SOURCES

1) _____   2) _____

Yosemite National Park

What is special about this popular California tourist destination? Why has the US Government set aside this land so that people can visit here and explore? Research online and share what you learn:

1 _____
2 _____
3 _____
4 _____

ONLINE SOURCES OF INFORMATION
⬇
_____

101 printable activities

C. Mahoney

Life is about choices...

Who is Thomas Jefferson?

Use a phone, tablet or laptop to learn five facts about this president and why he is remembered today.

1

2

3

4

5

6

7

ONLINE SOURCES OF INFORMATION:

1)	2)	3)

Israel

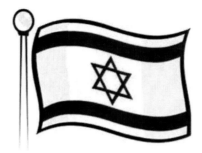

Use a phone, tablet or laptop to answer these questions.

1. What language do they speak? _____

2. How many people live there? _____

3. How big is this country? _____

4. Who is their leader? _____

5. Where is the capitol? _____

6. What kind of money do they use? _____

7. How long have they been a nation? _____

8. What religions are most common? _____

9. What sport is most popular? _____

10. What are three interesting things you learned? _____
_____
_____
_____
_____
_____
_____
_____
_____

SOURCE: _____
SOURCE: _____
SOURCE: _____

The California Flag

Search for facts about the California flag: the bear, the star, and the words "California" and "Republic". Why are they there and what do they signify?

1

2

3

4

ONLINE SOURCES OF INFORMATION:

What does it take to become a genius?

Use a <u>computer</u>, <u>tablet</u> or <u>phone</u> to search online for answers to this question.

1 ....

2 ....

3 ....

4 ....

5 ....

ONLINE SOURCES OF INFORMATION:

_____

_____

Big Buildings in America

Use a phone, tablet or laptop to answer these questions.

1. How big is the biggest HOUSE? _____

_____

SOURCE: _____

2. How big is the biggest HOTEL? _____

_____

SOURCE: _____

3. How big is the biggest CHURCH? _____

_____

SOURCE: _____

4. How big is the biggest HOSPITAL? _____

_____

SOURCE: _____

5. How big is the biggest PARKING LOT? _____

_____

SOURCE: _____

6. How big is the biggest SHOPPING MALL? _____

_____

SOURCE: _____

Alaska's Map

Use a phone, tablet or laptop to identify important places in this state: **mountains**, **rivers**, **lakes**, **cities**, **historical sites**, a neighboring **country, or** bordering bodies of **water**.

Birds

Use a phone, tablet or laptop to answer these questions.

What is the smallest bird?

_____
_____
_____
_____

What is the biggest bird?

_____
_____
_____

What is the fastest bird?

_____
_____
_____
_____

Which bird lives the longest?

_____
_____
_____
_____

source: _____
source: _____
source: _____
source: _____

Sea Critters

Use a phone, tablet or laptop to find an interesting fact about the **crab, lobster, penguin, angel fish, seal,** and **lion fish**

_____

_____

_____

_____

_____

_____

_____

_____

_____

_____

_____

_____

_____

_____

_____

_____

_____

_____

_____

_____

_____

_____

_____

_____

New Mexico

Use a phone, tablet or laptop to discover seven interesting facts about Mexico.

1

2

3

4

5

6

7

Sources:

The Lobster

Use a phone, tablet or laptop to answer these questions.

What it eats…

Fact #1: _____

_____

Fact #2: _____

_____

SOURCE: _____

Where it lives…

Fact #1: _____

_____

Fact #2: _____

_____

SOURCE: _____

Family life…

Fact #1: _____

_____

Fact #2: _____

_____

SOURCE: _____

Connection to humans…

Fact #1: _____

_____

Fact #2: _____

_____

SOURCE: _____

Israel's Language

English	Hebrew
hello	_____
goodbye	_____
bathroom	_____
water	_____
food	_____
help	_____
hospital	_____
police	_____
hotel	_____
me	_____
you	_____
airport	_____
taxi	_____
restaurant	_____
school	_____
office	_____
coffee	_____
computer	_____
telephone	_____
shoe	_____
umbrella	_____
book	_____
library	_____

The State Seal of Alaska

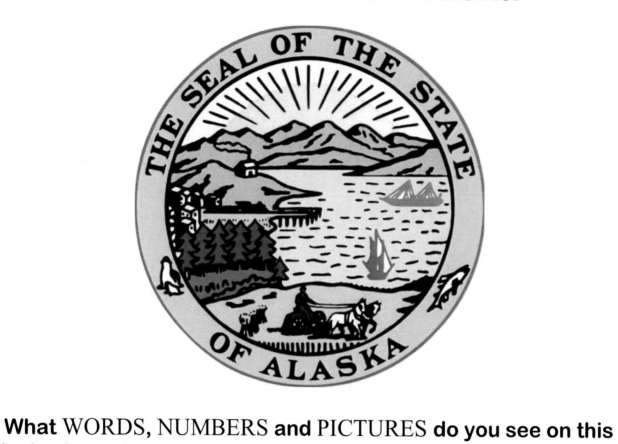

What WORDS, NUMBERS and PICTURES do you see on this Alaska State Seal and what does each represent? Search online for answers.

_____
_____
_____
_____
_____
_____
_____
_____
_____
_____
_____
_____
_____

Becoming a scientist

What does it take to become a scientist?
Use a <u>computer</u>, <u>tablet</u> or <u>phone</u> to search online for answers to this question.

1 ....
....
....

2 ....
....
....

3 ....
....
....

4 ....
....
....

5 ....
....
....

ONLINE SOURCES OF INFORMATION:

1)	2)	3)

Ohio's Geography

Use a phone, tablet or laptop to identify important places in this state: **mountains, rivers, lakes, cities, historical sites, neighboring states** or **bordering bodies of water**.

Height Records

Use a phone, tablet or laptop to answer these questions.

1. What is the tallest **building** in the world? _____

    _____

    source #1: _____

    source #2: _____

2. What is the tallest **mountain** in the world? _____

    _____

    source #1: _____

    source #2: _____

3. What is the tallest **waterfall** in the world? _____

    _____

    source #1: _____

    source #2: _____

4. What is the tallest **flagpole** in the world? _____

    _____

    source #1: _____

    source #2: _____

5. Who is the tallest **man** in the world? _____

    _____

    source #1: _____

    source #2: _____

6. Who is the tallest **woman** in the world? _____

    _____

    source #1: _____

    source #2: _____

Interesting Facts about Albert Einstein

Use a <u>computer</u>, <u>tablet</u> or <u>phone</u> to search online for information about this well-known scientist.

1

2

3

4

5

6

7

8

9

10

ONLINE SOURCES OF INFORMATION:

_____

_____

Forklifts

Use a phone, tablet or laptop to answer these questions.

1. How HEAVY is a forklift? _____

_____

SOURCE: _____

2. How FAST is a forklift? _____

_____

SOURCE: _____

3. How much can a forklift LIFT? _____

_____

SOURCE: _____

4. What are forklifts MADE of? _____

_____

SOURCE: _____

5. Why does the forklift make a BEEPING sound? _____

_____

SOURCE: _____

6. Who INVENTED the forklift? _____

_____

SOURCE: _____

Geography of the Europe

Use a phone, tablet or laptop to identify some of the largest and most populous countries in Europe:

Austria, Azerbaijan, Belarus, Belgium, Bulgaria, Croatia, Czech Republic, Denmark, England, Finland, France, Russia, Greece, Hungary, Ireland, Kazakhstan, Italy, Netherlands, Norway, Poland, Portugal, Romania, Scotland, Serbia, Slovakia, Spain, Sweden, Switzerland, Turkey, Ukraine, Wales

Who is Ronald Reagan?

Use a laptop, tablet or phone to access the internet and explore this California politician.

Age:

Gender:

Place of birth:

Ethnicity:

Political affiliation:

Job title:

Search for four interesting facts that you learned about them in your research:

The Mojave Tribe

What is special about this indigenous tribe of California? Go online and search for information about their <u>history</u> and <u>people</u>, their <u>religion</u> and where they <u>lived</u>, their <u>leaders</u> and the <u>language</u> they spoke.

1. _____
_____
_____
SOURCE: _____

2. _____
_____
_____
SOURCE: _____

3. _____
_____
_____
SOURCE: _____

The Caribbean Islands

Use a phone, tablet or laptop to identify some of the largest and most populous countries in the Caribbean:

Aruba, the Bahamas, Barbados, Cuba, Curacao, Cayman Islands, Dominican Republic, Grenada, Haiti, Jamaica, Martinique, Puerto Rico, Saint Lucia, Trinidad and Tobago, U.S. Virgin Islands

Who is Marcus Allen?

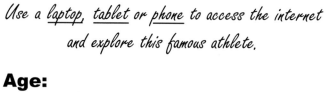

Use a laptop, tablet or phone to access the internet and explore this famous athlete.

Age:

Gender:

Place of birth:

Ethnicity:

Search for interesting facts about this famous athlete: major accomplishments in life, odd jobs, family and marriage, childhood experiences, accidents, anything that you find odd or strange:

_____

_____

_____

_____

_____

_____

_____

_____

_____

_____

_____

ONLINE SOURCES OF INFORMATION:

⬇

_____

_____

Germany's Money

Search online for an interesting coin from Germany. Use colored pencils, crayons or markers as you draw this coin. Be neat and accurate.

The State Seal of Hawaii

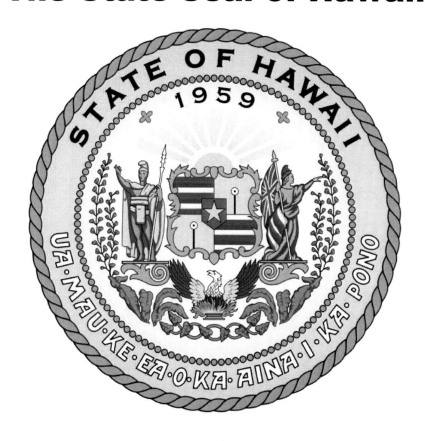

What WORDS, NUMBERS and PICTURES do you see on this Hawaii stamp and what does each represent? Search online for answers.

_____

_____

_____

_____

_____

_____

_____

_____

_____

The Iguana

Use a phone, tablet or laptop to answer these questions.

Is the iguana dangerous to humans?

☐ – YES

☐ – NO

How does an iguana eat?

Is an iguana smart?

YES NO

How long does an iguana live?

24 365 7

ONLINE SOURCES OF INFORMATION:

1)

2)

3)

Ohio's Flag

Draw the **state flag** of Ohio. Use colored pencils, crayons, or markers. Be neat and accurate.

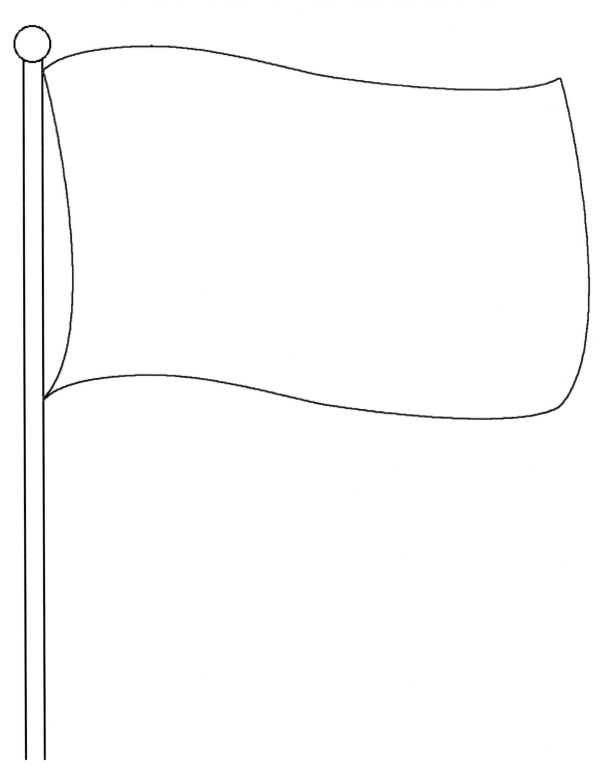

The Modoc Tribe

What is special about this indigenous tribe of California? Go online and search for information about their <u>history</u> and <u>people</u>, their <u>religion</u> and where they <u>lived</u>, their <u>leaders</u> and the <u>language</u> they spoke.

ONLINE SOURCES OF INFORMATION:

_____

_____

California Poppy Day

California State Holiday

Use a <u>laptop</u>, <u>tablet</u> or <u>phone</u> to access the internet and explore this **holiday**. Record several interesting facts you discovered in your research.

1._____
_____
_____
    SOURCE: _____

2._____
_____
_____
    SOURCE: _____

3._____
_____
_____
    SOURCE: _____

4._____
_____
_____
    SOURCE: _____

Famous People from Germany

_____

_____

_____

_____

_____

_____

_____

_____

_____

_____

_____

_____

_____

_____

_____

_____

_____

_____

_____

_____

_____

_____

_____

California Dogface Butterfly

California State Insect

Use a <u>laptop</u>, <u>tablet</u> or <u>phone</u> to access the internet and explore this **insect**. Record several interesting facts you discovered in your research.

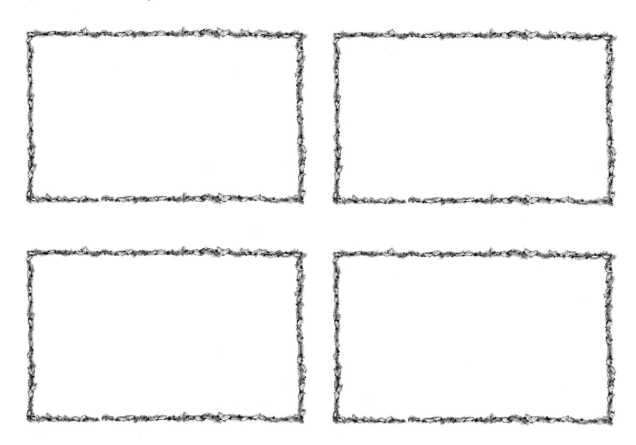

ONLINE SOURCES OF INFORMATION:

1)

2)

3)

Who is Jeff Gordon?

Use a laptop, tablet or phone to access the internet and explore this famous driver.

Age:

Gender:

Place of birth:

Ethnicity:

Search for interesting facts about this famous driver: major accomplishments in life, odd jobs, family and marriage, childhood experiences, accidents, anything that you find odd or strange:

_____

_____

_____

_____

_____

_____

_____

_____

_____

_____

_____

ONLINE SOURCES OF INFORMATION:

⬇

_____

_____

The State Seal of Ohio

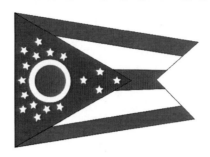

Draw the **Seal** or **Coat of Arms** for this state. Use colored pencils, crayons, or markers. Be neat and accurate.

The Indigenous Peoples of America

1.

2.

3.

4.

5.

6.

7.

8.

9.

10.

ONLINE SOURCES OF INFORMATION:

1)	2)	3)

Firetrucks

Use a phone, tablet or laptop to answer these questions.

1. How HEAVY is a firetruck? _____

_____

SOURCE: _____

2. How FAST is a firetruck? _____

_____

SOURCE: _____

3. How many PEOPLE can a firetruck carry? _____

_____

SOURCE: _____

4. Why are firetrucks RED? _____

_____

SOURCE: _____

5. How many WHEELS does a firetruck have? _____

_____

SOURCE: _____

6. Who INVENTED the firetruck? _____

_____

SOURCE: _____

Yosemite National Park

What is special about this popular California tourist destination? Why has the US Government set aside this land so that people can visit here and explore? Research online and share what you learn:

1

2

3

4

ONLINE SOURCES OF INFORMATION:

A Stamp from Germany

Search online for an interesting stamp from Germany. Use colored pencils, crayons or markers as you draw this stamp. Be neat and accurate.

Historical Facts about Texas

Use a phone, tablet or laptop to discover interesting facts about the history of Texas: wars, disasters, laws, accomplishments, challenges...

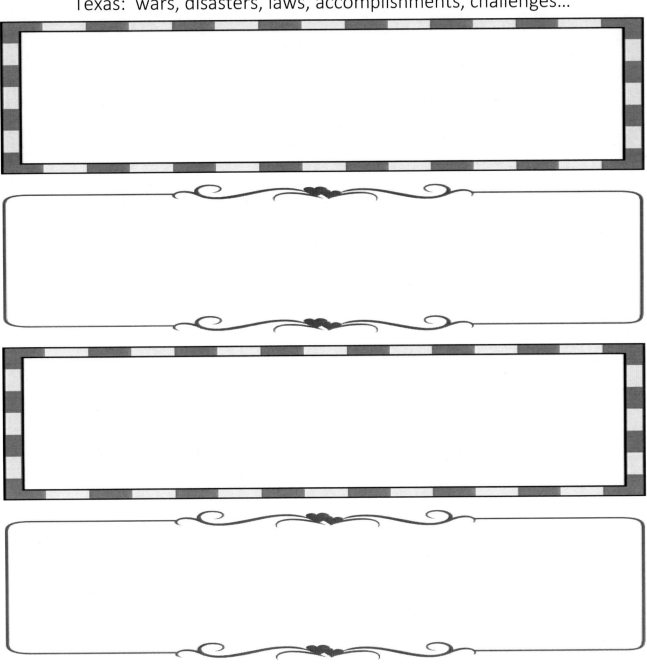

Birds

Use a phone, tablet or laptop to find an interesting fact about the **falcon**, **crow**, **peacock**, **penguin**, **seagull**, and **roadrunner**.

_____
_____
_____
_____

_____
_____
_____
_____

_____
_____
_____
_____

_____
_____
_____
_____

_____
_____
_____
_____

_____
_____
_____
_____

Internet Research on Ireland

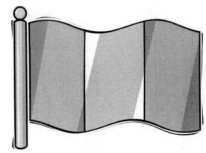

Use a phone, tablet or laptop to answer these questions.

1. What language do they speak? _____
2. How many people live there? _____
3. How big is this country? _____
4. Who is their leader? _____
5. Where is the capitol? _____
6. What kind of money do they use? _____
7. How long have they been a nation? _____
8. What religions are most common? _____
9. What sport is most popular? _____

10. What are three interesting things you learned? _____
_____
_____
_____
_____
_____
_____
_____
_____

SOURCE: _____
SOURCE: _____
SOURCE: _____

Searching for Gold

What is it like <u>sleeping</u> and <u>eating</u> and using the <u>restroom</u> while panning for gold in the mountains of California? Was it rough or easy? How did they survive the snowy winters and the rainy springs?

1

2

3

4

ONLINE SOURCES OF INFORMATION:

New York's Flag

Draw the **state flag** of New York. Use colored pencils, crayons, or markers. Be neat and accurate.

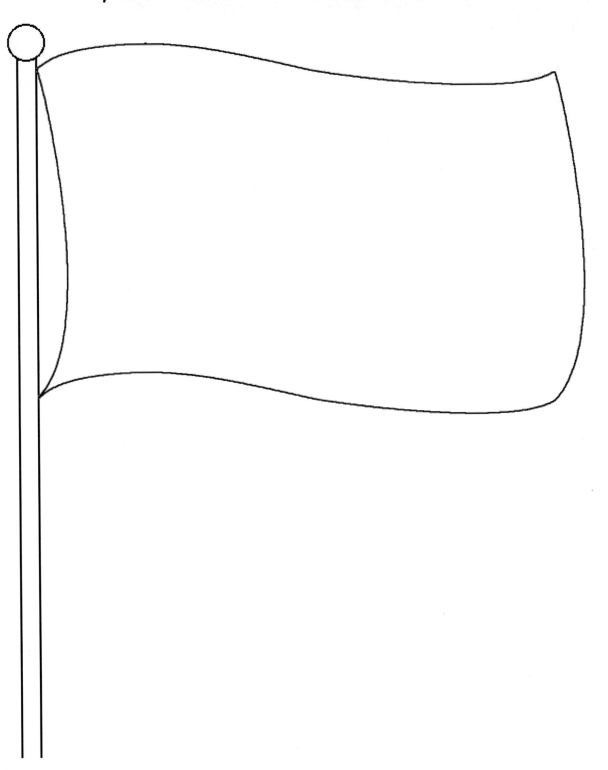

Water Mammals

Use a phone, tablet or laptop to answer these questions.

How long does this animal live?

Blue Whale: _____

Dolphin: _____

Seal: _____

Beaver: _____

Where is this animal is born?

Seal: _____

Polar Bear: _____

Dolphin: _____

Leopard Seal: _____

What does this animal eat?

Otter: _____

Orca: _____

Sea Lion: _____

Dolphin: _____

What covers the outside of this animal?

Dolphin: _____

Beaver: _____

Gray Whale: _____

Seal: _____

National Parks

Search online for ten interesting facts about national parks.

1.

2.

3.

4.

5.

6.

7.

8.

9.

10.

ONLINE SOURCES OF INFORMATION:

_____

_____

Who is Levi Strauss?

How did this man become rich during the Gold Rush? Write four facts about him and his choices.

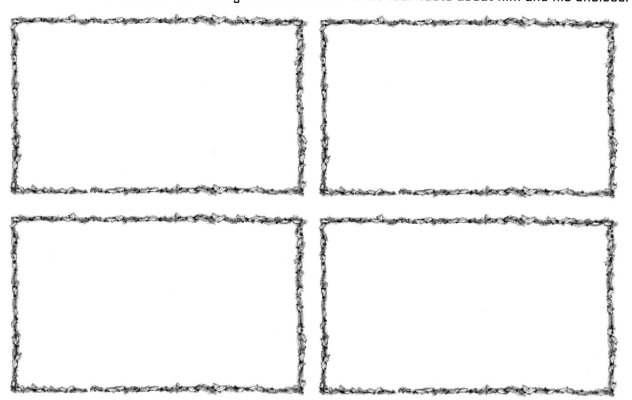

ONLINE SOURCES OF INFORMATION:

_____

_____

U.S. Stamp honoring Ohio

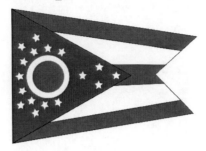

Search online for an interesting **stamp** honoring Ohio. Use colored pencils, crayons or markers as you draw this stamp. Be neat and accurate.

Animals with Wings

Use a phone, tablet or laptop to answer these questions.

How long does this animal live?

Raven:_____

Goose: _____

Barn Owl: _____

Praying Mantis: _____

Where is this animal is born?

Emperor Penguin: _____

Parrot: _____

Wasp: _____

Arctic Tern: _____

What does this animal eat?

Flamingo: _____

Dragonfly: _____

Toucan:_____

Crane: _____

What covers the outside of this animal?

Flying Fish: _____

Bat: _____

Penguin: _____

Honeybee: _____

Ohio

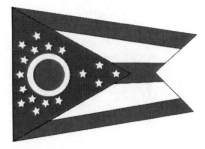

Use a phone, tablet or laptop to answer these questions.

1. What is the state motto? _____

2. How many people live there? _____

3. How big is this state? _____

4. Who is the governor? _____

5. Where is the capitol? _____

6. Which city is the largest? _____

7. How long have they been a state? _____

8. What job or work is most common? _____

9. What religion is most popular? _____

10. What are three interesting things you learned? _____

_____

_____

_____

_____

_____

_____

_____

_____

SOURCE: _____

SOURCE: _____

SOURCE: _____

Puerto Rico's Culture

Use a phone, tablet or laptop to discover interesting facts about this country.

Food

Music

Clothing

Sports

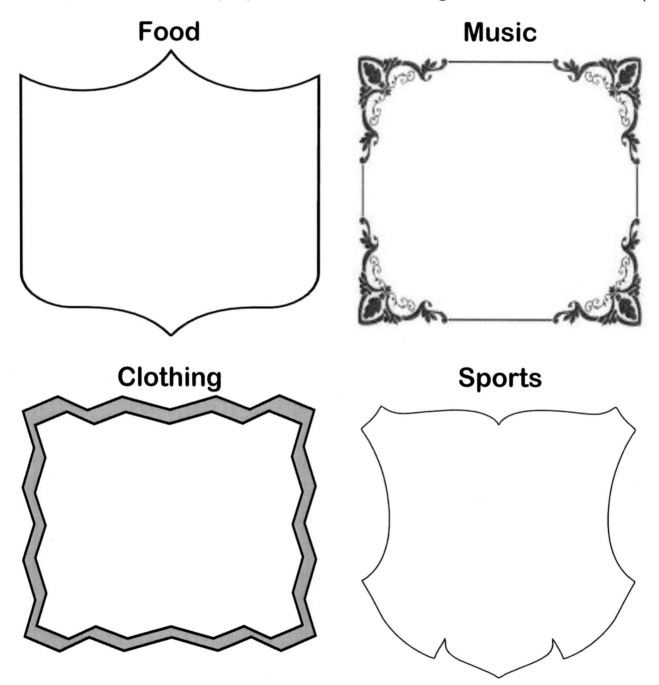

Germany's Language

English	German
hello	_____
goodbye	_____
bathroom	_____
water	_____
food	_____
help	_____
hospital	_____
police	_____
hotel	_____
me	_____
you	_____
airport	_____
taxi	_____
restaurant	_____
school	_____
office	_____
coffee	_____
computer	_____
telephone	_____
shoe	_____
umbrella	_____
book	_____
library	_____

Ohio's Wild Animals

Search online for information about the wild animals of Ohio (mammals, reptiles, birds and fish).

1 _____
_____
_____

2 _____
_____
_____

3 _____
_____
_____

ONLINE SOURCES OF INFORMATION:

_____
_____

The Quarter

Search online for information about the U.S. quarter (what is it made of, who is on it, how much does it cost to make it, where is it made, etc).

_____

_____

_____

_____

_____

_____

_____

_____

_____

_____

_____

ONLINE SOURCES OF INFORMATION:

1)

2)

3)

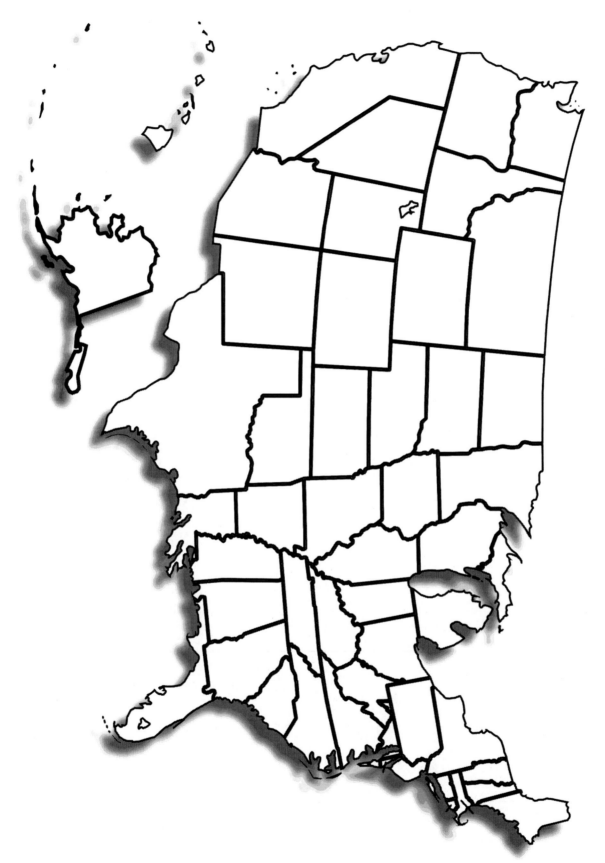

Use a phone, tablet or laptop to identify the 50 US states.

Countries in Asia

Use a phone, tablet or laptop to identify some of the largest and most populous countries in Asia:

Afghanistan, Bangladesh, China, Cambodia, Hong Kong, India, Indonesia, Iran, Iraq, Isreal, Japan, Jordan, Kazakhstan, Laos, Lebanon, Malyasia, Mongolia, Myanmar, Nepal, North Korea, Oman, Pakistan, Philippines, Qatar, Russia, Saudi Arabia, Singapore, South Korea, Syria, Taiwan, Thailand, Turkey, United Arab Empirates, Uzbekistan, Vietnam, Yemen

Food

Use a phone, tablet or laptop to answer these questions.

1. How big is the biggest APPLE? _____

_____

SOURCE: _____

2. How big is the biggest PIZZA? _____

_____

SOURCE: _____

3. How big is the biggest SANDWICH? _____

_____

SOURCE: _____

4. How big is the biggest CAKE? _____

_____

SOURCE: _____

5. How big is the biggest BURRITO? _____

_____

SOURCE: _____

6. How big is the biggest COOKIE? _____

_____

SOURCE: _____

Famous People from Israel

_____
_____
_____
_____
_____
_____
_____
_____
_____
_____
_____
_____
_____
_____
_____
_____
_____
_____
_____
_____
_____
_____
_____

The Cliffs of Moher

Search for interesting facts about this Irish tourist destination. What are its most interesting features? Why do people travel there and explore? What is so amazing about this place?

ONLINE SOURCES OF INFORMATION:

Interesting Facts about Russia

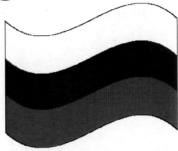

Use a phone, tablet or laptop to discover eight interesting facts.

1

2

3

4

5

6

7

8

Sources: _____

_____

Geography of China

Use a phone, tablet or laptop to identify important places in this country.

Mountains: _____

Rivers: _____

Lakes: _____

Oceans: _____

Cities: _____

_____

Historical sites: _____

_____

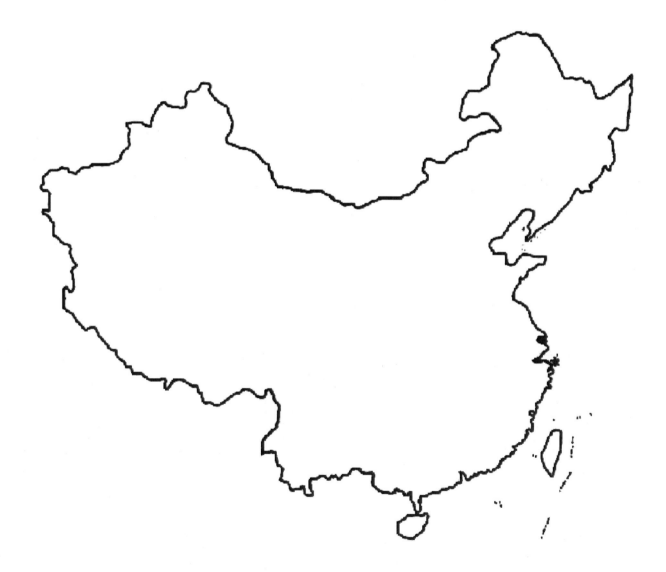

New York's Buildings

Search online for information about the skyscrapers in New York.

_____
_____
_____
_____
_____
_____
_____
_____
_____
_____
_____
_____
_____

ONLINE SOURCES OF INFORMATION:

1)

2)

3)

The Gray Whale

Use a <u>laptop</u>, <u>tablet</u> or <u>phone</u> to access the internet and explore this **marine mammal**. Record several interesting facts you discovered in your research.

1

2

3

4

5

SOURCES:

Who is George Washington?

Use a phone, tablet or laptop to learn about the first U.S. president.

1

2

3

4

5

ONLINE SOURCES OF INFORMATION:

1)

2)

3)

Valentine's Day

Use a <u>laptop</u>, <u>tablet</u> or <u>phone</u> to access the internet and explore **Valentine's Day**. Record three interesting facts you learned about why we celebrate this holiday on February 14th.

Interesting Facts about Germany

Use a phone, tablet or laptop to discover eight interesting facts.

1 _____

2 _____

3 _____

4 _____

5 _____

6 _____

7 _____

8 _____

Sources: _____

_____

The Garibaldi
California State Marine Fish

Use a <u>laptop</u>, <u>tablet</u> or <u>phone</u> to access the internet and explore this **marine fish**. Record several interesting facts you discovered in your research.

1

2

3

4

5

SOURCES:

Who is Gregor Mendel?

Use a phone, tablet or laptop to learn five facts about this scientist and why he is remembered today.

①

②

③

④

⑤

SOURCES:

Interesting Facts about New York

Use a phone, tablet or laptop to discover seven facts about New York.

1
_____
_____
_____

2
_____
_____
_____

3
_____
_____
_____

4
_____
_____
_____

5
_____
_____
_____

6
_____
_____
_____

7
_____
_____
_____

Sources: _____
_____

U.S. Coin honoring Ohio

Search online for the **U.S. quarter** that honors Ohio. Use colored pencils, crayons or markers as you draw the back of this coin. Be neat and accurate.

Geography of the Africa

Use a phone, tablet or laptop to identify some of the largest and most populous countries in Africa:

Algeria, Angola, Camaroon, Chad, Congo, Egypt, Ethiopia, Ghana, Ivory Coast, Kenya, Liberia, Libya, Madagascar, Mali, Morocco, Mozambique, Niger, Nigeria, Rwanda, Senegal, Sierra Leone, Somalia, South Africa, Sudan, Tanzania, Uganda, Zaire, Zambia, and Zimbabwe

Who is Benjamin Franklin?

Use a phone, tablet or laptop to learn five facts about this scientist and why he is remembered today.

1

2

3

4

5

SOURCES:

Historical Facts about Germany

Use a phone, tablet or laptop to discover interesting facts about the history of Germany: wars, disasters, laws, accomplishments, challenges...

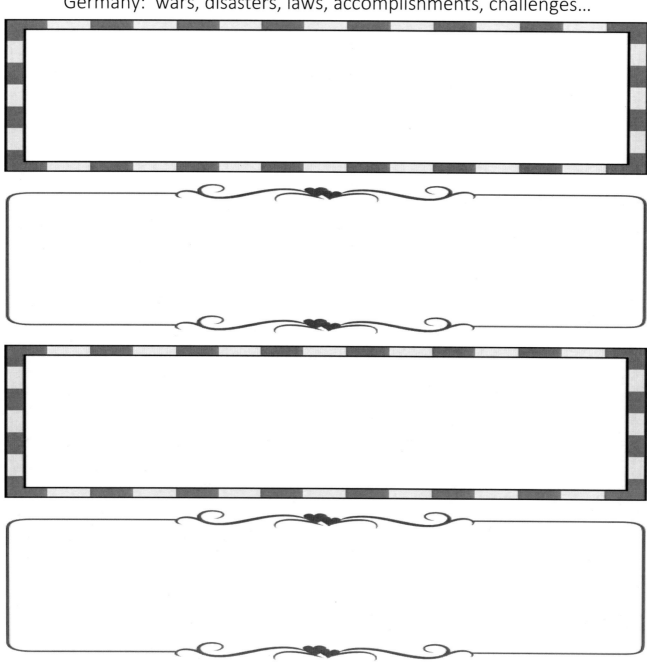

The Wildlife of Hawaii

Draw the state bird, tree, flower and insect of Hawaii. Use colored pencils, crayons, or markers. Be neat and accurate.

Bird

Tree

Flower

Insect

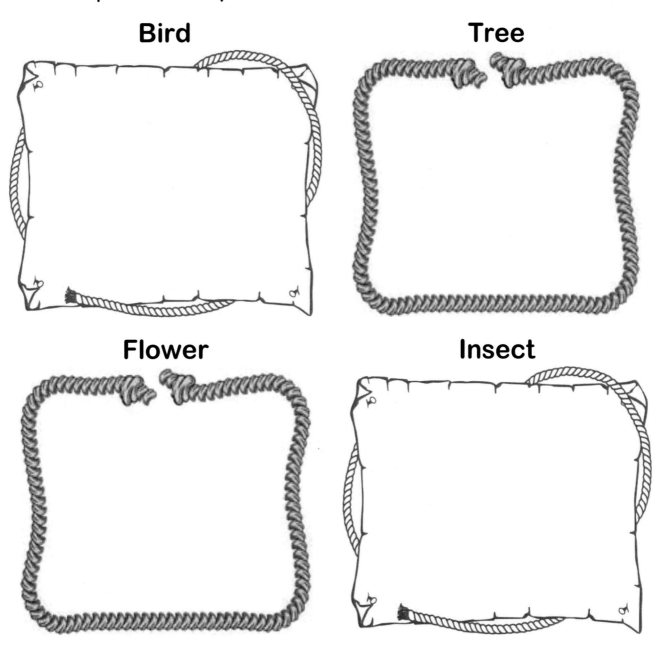

Geography of the North America

Use a phone, tablet or laptop to identify some of the largest and most populous countries in North America:

Belize, Canada, Costa Rica, Cuba, Dominican Republic, El Salvador, Greenland, Guatemala, Haiti, Honduras, Jamaica, Mexico, Nicaragua, Panama, United States of America,

Groundhog Day

Use a <u>laptop</u>, <u>tablet</u> or <u>phone</u> to access the internet and explore **Groundhog Day**. Record six interesting facts you learned about this holiday on February 2nd.

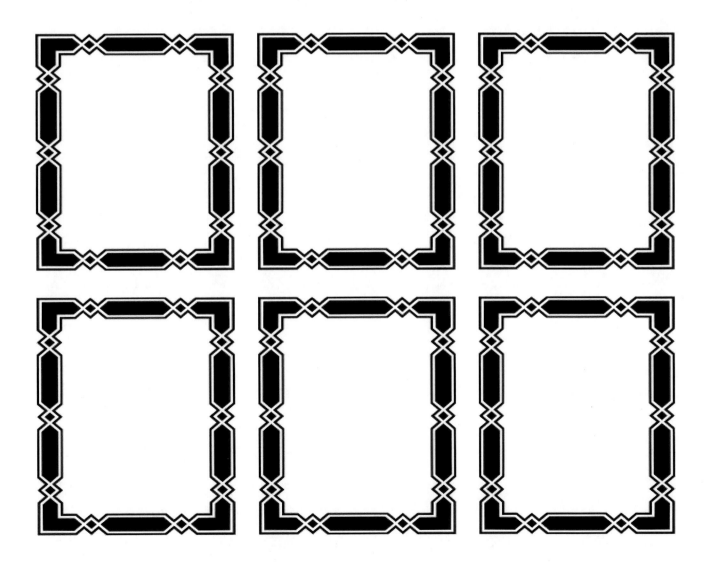

The Rattlesnake

Use a phone, tablet or laptop to answer these questions.

What it eats…

Fact #1: _____

_____

Fact #2: _____

_____

SOURCE: _____

Where it lives…

Fact #1: _____

_____

Fact #2: _____

_____

SOURCE: _____

Family life…

Fact #1: _____

_____

Fact #2: _____

_____

SOURCE: _____

Connection to humans…

Fact #1: _____

_____

Fact #2: _____

_____

SOURCE: _____

The Maidu Tribe

What is special about this indigenous tribe of California? Go online and search for information about their <u>history</u> and <u>people</u>, their <u>religion</u> and where they <u>lived</u>, their <u>leaders</u> and the <u>language</u> they spoke.

1

2

3

4

5

ONLINE SOURCES OF INFORMATION:

1)	2)	3)

Who is Mark McGwire?

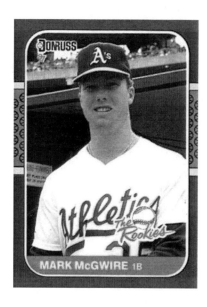

MARK McGWIRE 1B

Use a laptop, tablet or phone to access the internet and explore this famous athlete.

Age:

Gender:

Place of birth:

Ethnicity:

Search for interesting facts about this famous athlete: major accomplishments in life, odd jobs, family and marriage, childhood experiences, accidents, anything that you find odd or strange:

 1

 2

 3

 4

ONLINE SOURCES OF INFORMATION:

Geography of the Latin America

Use a phone, tablet or laptop to identify 22 Latin American countries:

Argentina, Belize, Bolivia, Brazil, Chile, Colombia, Costa Rica, Dominican Republic, Ecuador, El Salvador, French Guiana, Guatemala, Guyana, Honduras, Mexico, Nicaragua, Panama, Paraguay, Peru, Suriname, Uruguay, and Venezuela

Things I learned about Texas

Use a phone, tablet or laptop to learn interesting facts about Texas.

_____

_____

_____

_____

_____

_____

_____

_____

_____

_____

_____

_____

_____

_____

_____

_____

_____

_____

_____

_____

_____

_____

_____

_____

Sources: _____

_____

Ohio's Wildlife

Draw the state bird, tree, flower and insect of Ohio. Use colored pencils, crayons, or markers. Be neat and accurate.

Bird

Tree

Flower

Insect

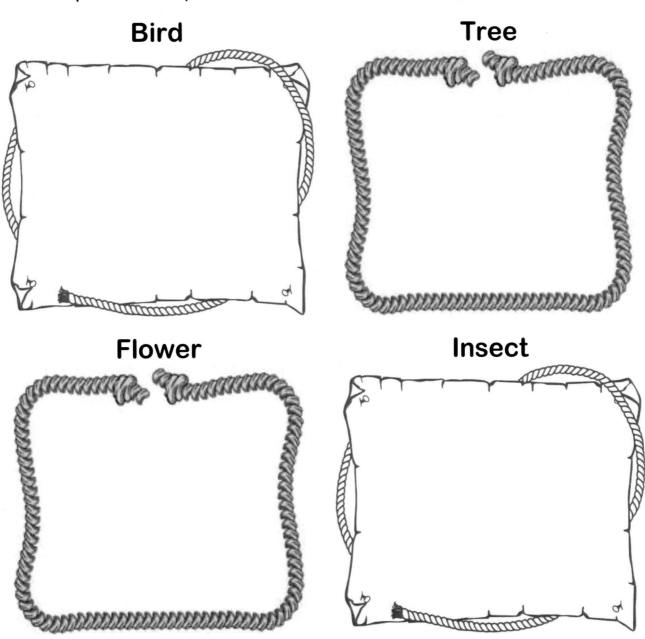

What is the job of an actor?

List ten activities or actions that a politician is responsible for:

1.

2.

3.

4.

5.

6.

7.

8.

9.

10.

ONLINE SOURCES OF INFORMATION:

_____

_____

China's Culture

Use a phone, tablet or laptop to discover interesting facts about this country.

Food

Music

Clothing

Sports

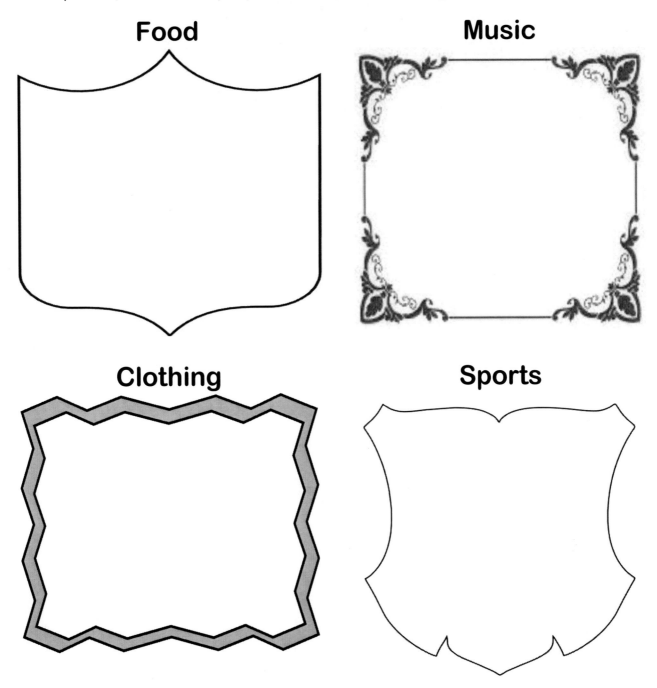

Love Your Pet Day

Use a <u>laptop</u>, <u>tablet</u> or <u>phone</u> to access the internet and explore **pets**. Record five interesting facts you learned about this celebration on February 20th.

The Yurok Tribe

What is special about this indigenous tribe of California? Go online and search for information about their <u>history</u> and <u>people</u>, their <u>religion</u> and where they <u>lived</u>, their <u>leaders</u> and the <u>language</u> they spoke.

_____

_____

_____

_____

_____

_____

_____

_____

_____

_____

_____

_____

ONLINE SOURCES OF INFORMATION:

⬇

_____

_____

The Spider

Use a phone, tablet or laptop to answer these questions.

1. How small is the world's smallest spider? _____

_____

_____

source #1: _____

source #2: _____

2. How large is the world's largest spider? _____

_____

_____

source #1: _____

source #2: _____

3. What do spiders eat? _____

_____

_____

source #1: _____

source #2: _____

4. What happens if a spider loses a leg? _____

_____

_____

source #1: _____

source #2: _____

5. How does a spider learn to capture prey? _____

_____

_____

source #1: _____

source #2: _____

Presidio of San Francisco

What is special about this popular California tourist destination? Why has the US Government set aside this land so that people can visit here and explore? Research online and share what you learn:

ONLINE SOURCES OF INFORMATION:

Ohio's Culture

Use a phone, tablet or laptop to discover interesting facts about this state.

Food

Music

Clothing

Sports

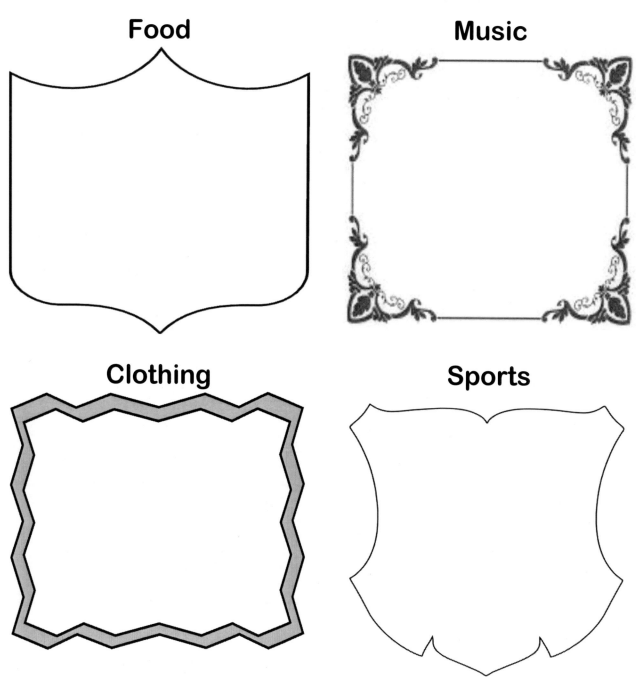

Redwood National Park

What is special about this popular California tourist destination? Why has the US Government set aside this land so that people can visit here and explore? Research online and share what you learn:

 1

 2

 3

 4

ONLINE SOURCES OF INFORMATION:

Israel's Flag

Draw the national flag of Israel. Use colored pencils, crayons, or markers. Be neat and accurate.

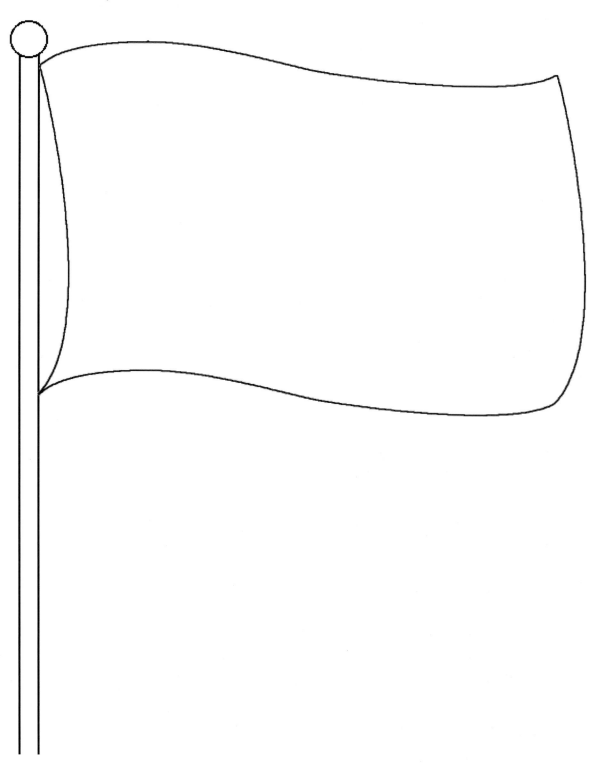

Mammals

Use a phone, tablet or laptop to find an interesting fact about these mammals.

_____
_____
_____
_____

_____
_____
_____
_____

_____
_____
_____
_____

_____
_____
_____
_____

_____
_____
_____
_____

_____
_____
_____
_____

The Coyote

Use a phone, tablet or laptop to answer these questions.

Is the coyote dangerous to humans?

☐ – YES

☐ – NO

_____
_____
_____
_____

How does a coyote eat?

_____
_____
_____
_____

Is a coyote smart?

YES
OR
NO

_____
_____
_____
_____

How long does a coyote live?

_____
_____
_____
_____

24 7 365

source: _____

source: _____

source: _____

Protecting the Land

Search online for ten ways that we can protect the land and its natural inhabitants.

1.

2.

3.

4.

5.

6.

7.

8.

9.

10.

ONLINE SOURCES OF INFORMATION:

_____

_____

Geography of the Middle East

Use a phone, tablet or laptop to identify these countries of the Middle East:

Egypt, Iran, Turkey, Iraq, Saudi Arabia, Yemen, United Arab Emirates, Israel, Jordan, Palestine, Lebanon, Oman, Kuwait, Qatar, and Bahrain.

Lincoln's Birthday

Use a laptop, tablet or phone to access the internet and learn about **Abraham Lincoln**. Record several interesting facts you learned about the sixteenth President of the United States.

_____

_____

_____

_____

_____

_____

_____

_____

_____

_____

USA

The Desert Tortoise

Use a phone, tablet or laptop to answer these questions.

What it eats…

Fact #1: _____

_____

Fact #2: _____

_____

SOURCE: _____

Where it lives…

Fact #1: _____

_____

Fact #2: _____

_____

SOURCE: _____

Family life…

Fact #1: _____

_____

Fact #2: _____

_____

SOURCE: _____

Connection to humans…

Fact #1: _____

_____

Fact #2: _____

_____

SOURCE: _____

Historical Facts about Ohio

Use a phone, tablet or laptop to discover interesting facts about the history of Ohio: wars, disasters, laws, accomplishments, challenges...

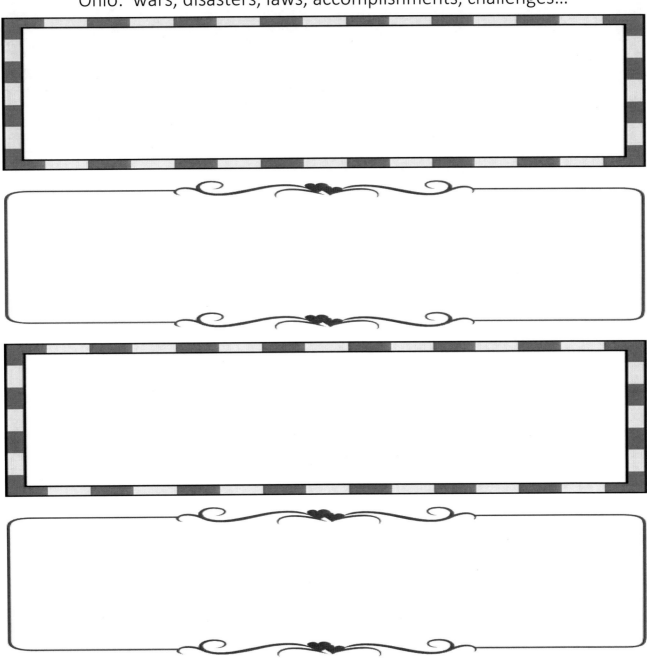

Washington's Birthday

Use a <u>laptop</u>, <u>tablet</u> or <u>phone</u> to access the internet and explore **George Washington**. Record five interesting facts you learned about the first President of the United States.

The Miwok Tribe

What is special about this indigenous tribe of California? Go online and search for information about their <u>history</u> and <u>people</u>, their <u>religion</u> and where they <u>lived</u>, their <u>leaders</u> and the <u>language</u> they spoke.

ONLINE SOURCES OF INFORMATION:

_____

_____

The Great Lakes

Search online for interesting facts about the Great Lakes.

What is the job of the President?

List ten activities or actions that a President is responsible for:

1.

2.

3.

4.

5.

6.

7.

8.

9.

10.

SOURCES:

_____

_____

The Mono Tribe

What is special about this indigenous tribe of California? Go online and search for information about their <u>history</u> and <u>people</u>, their <u>religion</u> and where they <u>lived</u>, their <u>leaders</u> and the <u>language</u> they spoke.

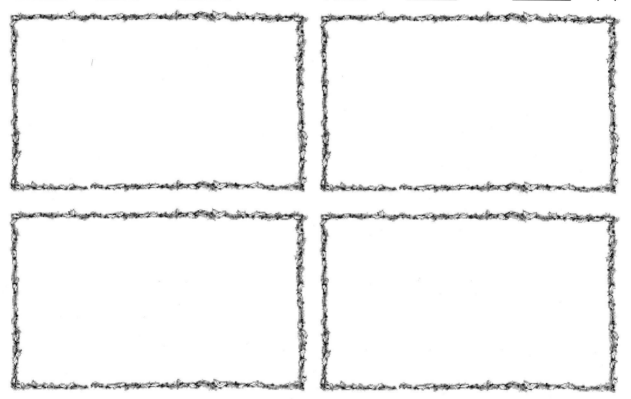

ONLINE SOURCES OF INFORMATION:

_____

_____

The Alamo

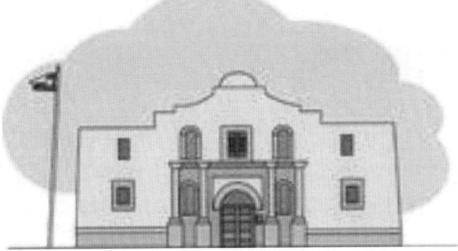

Search online for information about The Alamo.

Internet Safety

1

Do your work. Don't play around. You have an assignment to do, so focus your attention where it is supposed to be.

2

Search for answers to the questions. Don't get caught going down rabbit holes in search of weird or strange stuff.

3

Imagine that your mother is sitting on your right and your teacher is sitting on your left, watching what you're doing. What would they say to you right now? Make good choices.

This workbook is part of a series:

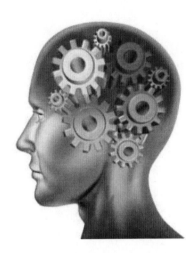

✓ Back to School Internet Research Projects (Grades 5-8)

✓ Christmas Vacation Internet Research Projects (Grades 5-8)

✓ Spring Break Internet Research Projects (Grades 5-8)

✓ End of School Internet Research Projects (Grades 5-8)

✓ Summer Vacation Internet Research Projects (Grades 5-8)

✓ Middle School Internet Research Projects (Grades 5-8)

✓ Junior High Internet Research Projects (Grades 5-8)

Each workbook is filled with 101 different activities to explore animals, people, foreign countries, U.S. states, athletes, singers, politicians, actors, holidays, Native Americans, postage stamps, coins, flags, maps, and so much more. All are available at Amazon.

Made in United States
North Haven, CT
03 October 2022

24973069R00059